Clean and Healthy

Angela Royston

Heinemann LIBRARY

www.heinemann.co.uk

Visit our website to find out more information about **Heinemann Library** books.

To order:

☎ Phone 44 (0) 1865 888066

▤ Send a fax to 44 (0) 1865 314091

▢ Visit the Heinemann Bookshop at www.heinemann.co.uk to browse our catalogue and order online.

First published in Great Britain by
Heinemann Library,
Halley Court, Jordan Hill, Oxford OX2 0EJ,
a division of Reed Educational and Professional
Publishing Ltd.
Heinemann is a registered trademark of Reed
Educational & Professional Publishing Limited.

OXFORD MELBOURNE AUCKLAND
JOHANNESBURG BLANTYRE GABORONE
IBADAN PORTSMOUTH NH (USA) CHICAGO

© Reed Educational and Professional Publishing
Ltd 1999
The moral right of the proprietor has been
asserted.

Designed by Celia Floyd
Printed and bound in Hong Kong/China

ISBN 0 431 09146 3 (hardback)
03 02 01 00
10 9 8 7 6 5 4 3 2

ISBN 0 431 09147 1 (paperback)
03 02 01 00
10 9 8 7 6 5 4 3 2 1

British Library Cataloguing in Publication Data

Royston, Angela
   Clean and healthy. – (Safe and sound)
   1. Health – Juvenile literature 2. Hygiene –
   Juvenile literature
   I. Title
   631'.0432

Acknowledgements

The Publishers would like to thank the following
for permission to reproduce photographs: Bubbles:
Dr H Robinson pp28, 29, F Rombout p27; J Allan
Cash Ltd: p16; Trevor Clifford: pp5, 7, 8, 9, 10, 11, 12,
13, 14, 15, 18, 19, 20, 22, 23; Format: M Murray p17;
Carol Palmer: p25; Science Photo Library: M Clarke
pp21, 26, Dr L Stannard, UCT p6, H Young p24; Tony
Stone Images: P Cade p4.

Cover photograph reproduced with permission of
Trevor Clifford.

Every effort has been made to contact copyright
holders of any material reproduced in this book.
Any omissions will be rectified in subsequent
printings if notice is given to the Publisher.

The Publishers would like to thank Julie Johnson,
PSHE consultant and trainer, for her comments in
the preparation of this book.

Any words appearing in the text in bold, **like this**,
are explained in the Glossary.

Contents

Soap and water

When you play outside you may get muddy and grubby. When you come in you need to wash away the dirt, especially from your hands and face.

Washing protects you from **germs** that can make you unhealthy. In this book you will learn lots of ways to keep clean and healthy.

What are germs?

Germs are tiny living things. This is what they look like under a **microscope**. Germs are really thousands of times smaller than this – much too small to see without a microscope.

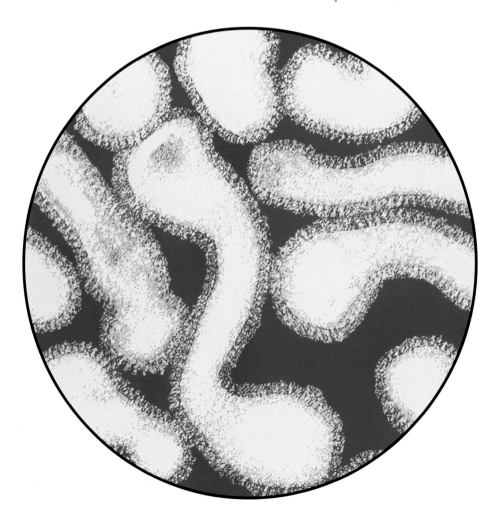

If germs get inside your body they can make you ill. Some germs give you flu and make you sneeze.

How germs spread

Germs can pass from one person to another.
When you have a cold, you breathe out germs
every time you sneeze, cough or breathe out!

Other people may breathe in some of your germs. Make sure you cover your mouth when you cough. This will stop the germs spreading through the air.

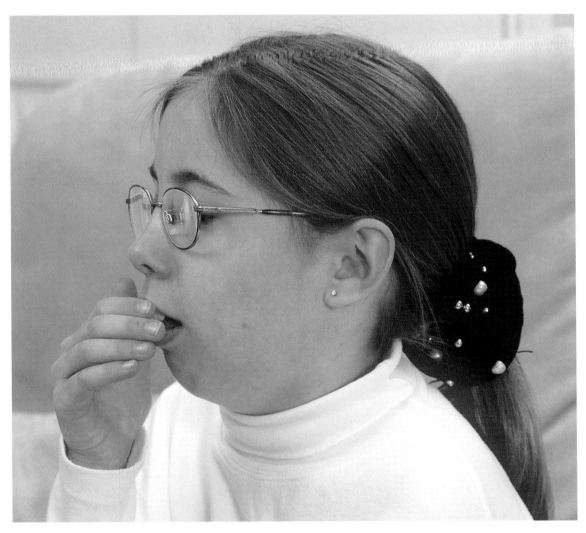

Wash your hands!

Lots of **germs** leave your body when you go to the toilet. Always wash your hands well afterwards. This will keep away **worms** as well as germs.

It is very easy for germs to spread from your hands into your mouth. Always wash your hands before you eat any food.

Clean Food

You may take in **germs** when you eat, drink or put something in your mouth. If food falls on the ground or gets dirty, throw it away.

There are germs everywhere, so be careful what you put in your mouth. Pens and pencils, even your thumb, may be covered with germs.

Pets

Pets are fun to play with. Cats, dogs and many other pets love to be stroked. But their fur and mouths may be full of **germs**.

This dog is very friendly, but don't let your pet lick your mouth.

Wild animals

Do you sometimes feed ducks and other birds? Remember, many wild animals have **fleas** and their **droppings** carry **germs**.

Some wild animals spread dangerous germs. Don't play near rubbish or on wasteground where there may be rats or other **pests** nearby.

Don't touch blood

Blood can carry dangerous **germs**. Never touch anyone else's blood. If your friend has a cut, give him or her some clean paper to put over it.

Always ask a grown-up to clean a cut. Put a plaster on to protect the **wound** and keep it clean while it heals.

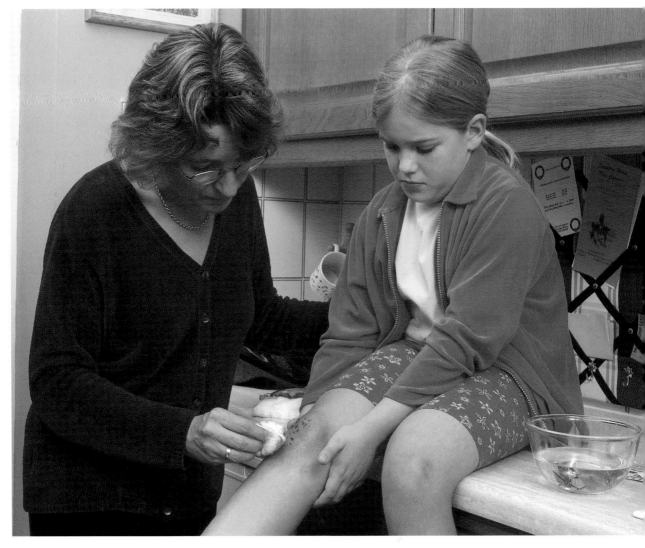

Hair care

Head lice are tiny insects that live in your hair. They won't hurt you, but they make your head itch. They can crawl from one person's hair to another.

Comb your hair every day with a special comb. Check to see if there are any head lice on it. If there are, you may need to use a special shampoo to get rid of them.

Brush your teeth!

You should brush your teeth at least twice a day!
Bits of food left in your mouth can turn into **acid**.
Acid makes holes in your teeth.

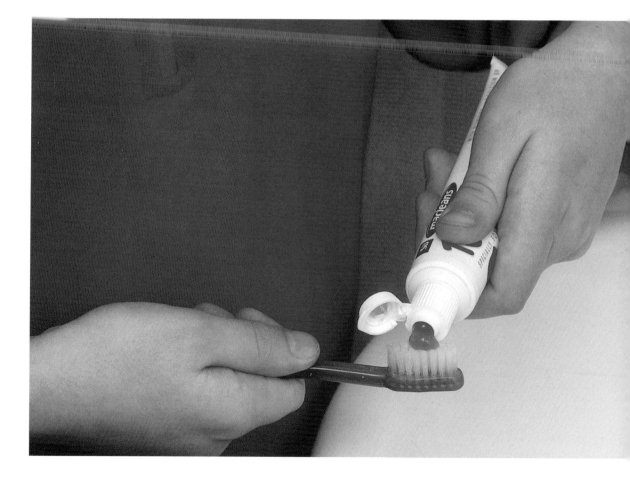

Make sure you brush the front and back of your teeth from the gums to the tips. Then brush the tops of the big teeth at the back of your mouth.

Visiting the dentist

You should visit the dentist every six months. The dentist checks to see if all your teeth are strong and healthy.

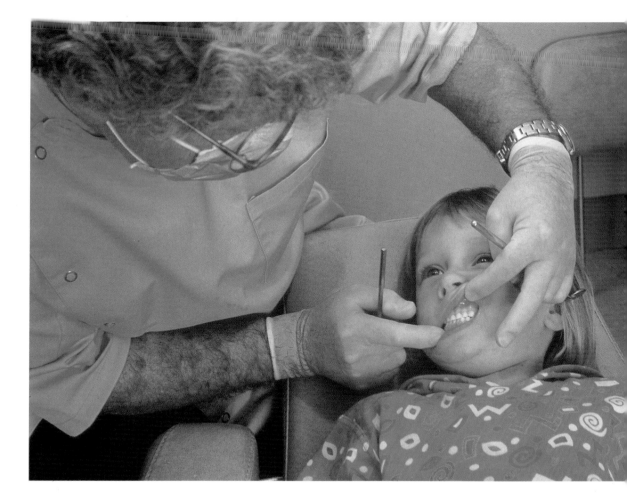

The dentist may remind you to clean your teeth night and morning. Remember to clean them after eating or drinking something sweet.

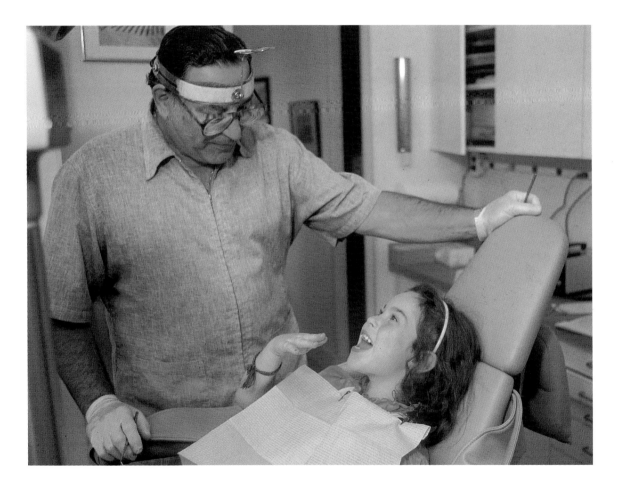

Visiting the doctor

A medical check helps to keep you healthy. A nurse may measure your weight and your height. Do you know how tall you are now?

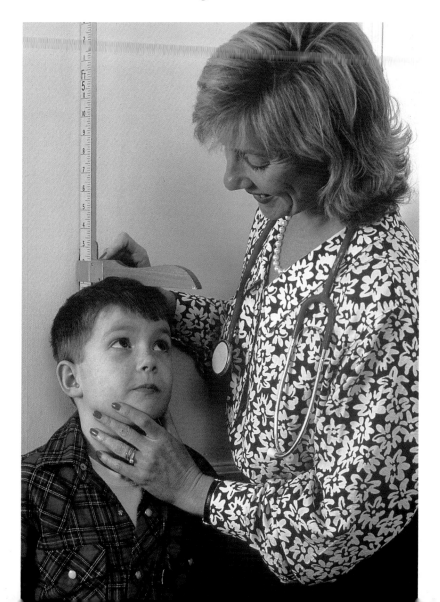

A doctor or nurse also checks how well you see and hear. Many people wear glasses to help them see more clearly.

Keeping well

Vaccinations stop you catching some serious illnesses. The **vaccines** help your body to fight and kill **diseases** before they make you ill.

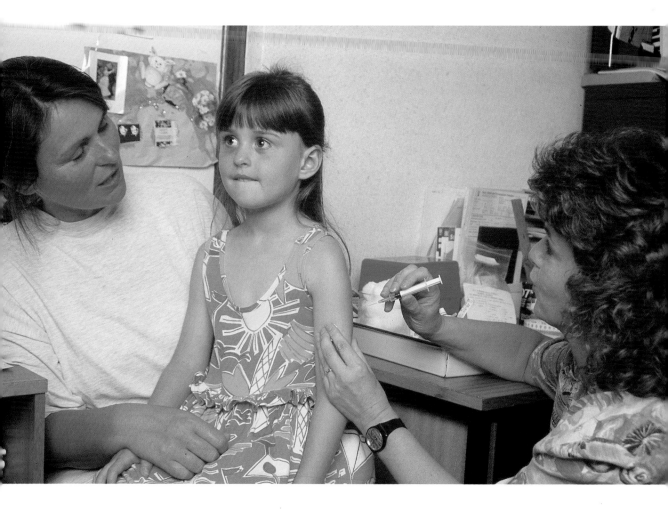

Many vaccines are **injected** from a needle through a prick in the skin. Some are dropped straight into your mouth. Now you are less likely to get ill!

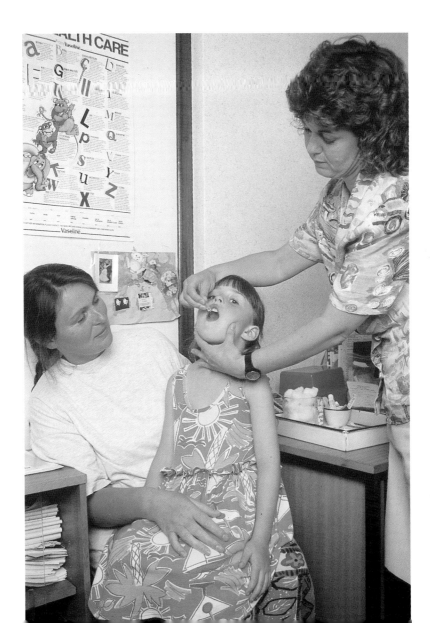

Glossary

acid   a sour-tasting liquid that can make holes in your teeth

blood   red liquid that carries food and oxygen around the body

disease   illness

dropping   animal dung

flea   tiny insect that lives on an animal's body

germ   tiny living thing that can get inside the body and make you ill

head louse   insect that lives in the hair. It lays eggs (called nits) on the hair close to the head.

injected   pushed in

microscope   a machine that makes things look much larger than they really are

pest   living thing that can cause damage or disease

vaccination   when a vaccine is given

vaccine   a small dose of dead or weak germs that the body can easily kill. The body is then always ready to kill germs before they can make you ill.

worm   small animal without bones or legs. Threadworms can live inside the intestines, which are the long tubes in your body that food goes into after it passes through the stomach.

wound   injury like a cut or a bruise, not caused by an illness

Index